The Social Work Pocket Guide to… Effective Supervision

By Siobhan Maclean

First Edition 2012 ISBN: 978-1-903575-80-2

A catalogue record for this book will be available from the British Lit

©Kirwin Maclean Associates Ltd 4 Mesnes Green, Lichfield, Staffs, WS

3

Contents List...

What?

Why?

How?

WHAT?

Effective practice is made up of knowledge, skills and values. Each of these components of practice effectively build upon each other. Seeking to develop skills without the necessary knowledge would therefore be futile. To develop effective practice in supervision, knowledge about the basic framework of supervision is important. This section of the pocket guide will therefore consider the following questions:

- What is supervision?
- What are the origins of supervision?
- What are the functions of supervision?
- What are the main forms and models of supervision in social work?

Working through these questions will help to set the foundations for the remainder of the Pocket Guide.

WHAT IS SUPERVISION ALL ABOUT?

Supervision is...

.... the key process for balancing professional autonomy with responsibility to the client, professional ethics and standards along with accountability to the agency and society at large.

(Stevenson 2005: 1)

..... focused on change, aiming at people who work professionally getting the opportunity to share their experiences and thoughts...... so that the supervisee will be more competent in her / his profession.

(Petitt and Olsson 1995)

.....a process by which one worker is given responsibility by the organisation to work with another worker(s) in order to meet certain organisational, professional and personal objectives which together promote the best outcomes for service users.

(Morrison 2005: 32)

What?

…..a process by which an organisation provides support and guidance to social workers.

(BASW 2011)

….a process which facilitates critical reflection upon actions, processes, persons and the context of social work practice.

(O'Donoghue 2000)

A container that holds the helping relationship within the 'therapeutic triad'.

(Hawkins and Shohet 2006: 3)

……an accountable process which supports, assures and develops the knowledge, skills and values of an individual, group or team. The purpose is to improve the quality of their work to achieve agreed objectives and outcomes.

(Childrens Workforce Development Council and Skills for Care 2007)

The objectives of supervision

It is generally accepted that there are four main objectives to supervision (for example see Morrison 2005):

1. Ensuring competent accountable practice

2. Encouraging continuing professional development

3. Offering personal support to practitioners

4. Engaging the individual practitioner with the organisation

The functions of supervision

The objectives of supervision are met through the main functions of supervision. Whilst different writers use different terms it is generally accepted that there are four main functions to social work supervision (which relate to the four objectives). These functions are often reflected in agency supervision policies.

Managerial function
This is also referred to as the accountability, administrative or normative function.

Developmental function
This is also referred to as the educative or formative function.

Supportive function
This is also referred to as the restorative or pastoral function.

Mediation function
This is also referred to as the negotiation function.

Managerial function

A key aspect of any form of social work supervision is that the supervisee is accountable to the supervisor for the work that they do. The Children's Workforce Development Council (2007: 4) clarify that *"Supervision is an accountable process."* Supervisors therefore need to utilise supervision to ensure that the supervisee is competent in their practice and to monitor the quality of service provision.

Freeth (2007) highlights the fact social work is pre-occupied with the managerial functions of supervision. Certainly, many of the social workers I speak to, feel that caseload management and managerialist issues dominate their experiences of supervision. Despite this pre-occupation with the managerial function, research by the British Association of Social Workers (2011) found that 58% of respondents felt that casework issues were not adequately dealt within their supervision.

What?

Developmental function

Supervisors sometimes misunderstand the developmental function and think that asking a question like *"What training have you been on?"* or *"What courses are you considering?"* means they have covered the developmental function!

However, supervision should be developmental in itself - it should enable a practitioner's learning by promoting adult learning processes and critically reflective practice. Supervisors should encourage practitioners to reflect on what they have learnt from their practice within all supervision discussion.

In research by the British Association of Social Workers (2011) 62% of respondents stated that their personal development was not adequately addressed in their supervision.

Supportive function

Supervision needs to provide a supportive forum where the supervisee can discuss their concerns and explore their emotional responses to their work.

Where supervision provides a supportive environment the other functions of supervision are more likely to be addressed. For example, Atkin and Weil (1981: 473) state that *"supportive supervision helps the supervisee to develop the ego strength needed to deal with the natural anxieties of the task at hand, and serves to remove road blocks to his or her personal development as an independent professional."*

Despite the central importance of this function it is perhaps one of the areas where social workers feel most 'let down'. In a recent survey of social workers (BASW 2011) 70% of respondents felt that the emotional issues arising from their work were not adequately addressed in supervision.

What?

Mediation function

This is the function of supervision which is least commonly written about. Many agency supervision policies reflect, or even specifically refer to, the first three functions of supervision, but most make little or no reference to the mediation function. Focussed on engaging the worker with the organisation, Morrison (2005: 46) asserts that the mediation function is about:

- Negotiating and clarifying team roles and responsibilities
- Briefing management about resource deficits or implications
- Allocating resources in the most efficient way
- Representing supervisees needs to higher management
- Consulting and briefing staff about organisational developments or information
- Mediating or advocating between workers, within the team or other parts of the agency or outside agencies

The origins of supervision

Regular readers of Social Work Pocket Guides will know that I like to research the origins of words to help me understand concepts more fully.

The word supervision is derived from two Latin words:

Super – which means over

Videre – which means to watch or to see

Literally taken then, the word supervision means "overseeing".

What?

The development of supervision

The roots of contemporary social work supervision lie in the growth of charitable social organisations in Europe and North America. These organisations engaged volunteer 'visitors' who were 'overseen' by a nominated 'overseer'.

In the very early part of the 20th Century as 'casework' practice became more common the beginnings of contemporary approaches to supervision took root. The first books on supervision began to appear - for example, "Supervision and Education in Charity" by Jeffrey Bracket was published in 1904.

Munson (2002) argues that the form and structure of supervision has remained fairly constant since the nineteenth century. However, some practitioners argue that managerialist approaches in contemporary social work have led to a regression to earlier forms of simple overseeing.

Forms of supervision

Supervision can take various forms. Every supervision session can be described as either:

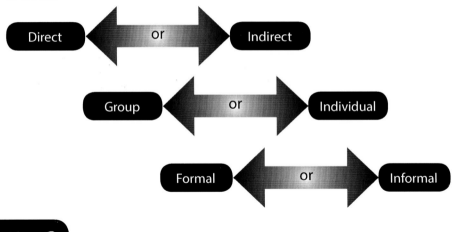

Direct — or — Indirect

Group — or — Individual

Formal — or — Informal

What?

Direct or Indirect

Supervision can be described as either direct or indirect. The concept of this can be misunderstood, such that I have heard managers referring to direct supervision as face to face contact and indirect supervision as phone discussions or advice provided through IT systems. This is an inaccurate understanding of the concept.

In other professions direct supervision is referred to as live supervision and this is probably the most helpful term. In fact, direct supervision refers to supervision which takes place 'on the job' – basically discussion, advice and direction whilst a practitioner is actually undertaking a task. Whilst direct supervision is regularly used in social care environments where staff are provided with on the job support, its use is less common in social work.

Most of the supervision we engage in within social work would be described as indirect – away from the actual work with specific time set aside for supervision and reflection.

Group or Individual

Although most supervisors will have responsibility for supervising more than one practitioner, the majority of supervision takes place on a one-to-one basis. However, group supervision (perhaps on a team or peer group basis) is becoming increasingly popular. For example, group supervision is commonly used in social work education. According to Lindsay (2003), whilst the move towards group supervision for students was driven by a lack of resources, students report many benefits to this form of supervision.

Group supervision addresses the functions of supervision by:

- developing individuals through peer / active learning
- providing a strong forum for managerial influence and mediation
- exerting pressure for change through group dynamics

Whilst group supervision is very positive it should compliment rather than replace individual supervision sessions.

What?

Formal or Informal

My view is that informal supervision describes the discussions / consultation which take place between supervisor and supervisee in between formal sessions. Sometimes informal supervision is seen as taking place outside of the supervisory relationship - for example, a practitioner consulting with a more experienced colleague is described by some as informal supervision. I would refer to this as consultation, or if this is a regular occurrence perhaps a mentoring relationship is developing.

There will always be a need for informal supervision in between planned formal supervision sessions. When a worker is new to a team, is undertaking a new area of work or a particular task, there is likely to be a need for more informal supervision.

Developmental models of supervision

Social work practice educators often utilise developmental models of supervision, which are mostly drawn from the literature around supervision in counselling. Developmental models generally refer to a practitioner progressing through several developmental stages which supervisors should take into account in providing supervision. All of the developmental models focus on how as a practitioner's experience develops, they become less dependent on the supervision relationship.

Developmental models can be particularly helpful in understanding how an individual responds to the supervisory relationship as they develop skills and become more confident in their practice. As such they can be particularly useful to supervisors of students and newly qualified workers.

What?

The basis of developmental models is outlined by Smith (undated online) as focussing on the development of practitioners and their use of supervision through four 'levels':

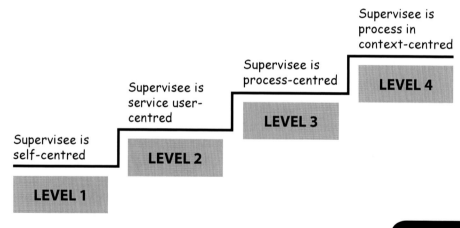

Supervisee is self-centred

LEVEL 1

Supervisee is service user-centred

LEVEL 2

Supervisee is process-centred

LEVEL 3

Supervisee is process in context-centred

LEVEL 4

The Dreyfus developmental model

Widely used in education, the Dreyfus model (1986) focuses on how people acquire skills and develop competence, moving through 5 stages from novice to expert.

Stage	Characteristics	Decision-making
Novice	- rigid adherence to rules - lack of discretionary judgement	Laboured and often reliant on others
Advanced beginner	- limited situational perception - all aspects of work treated separately with equal importance	Sometimes reliant on others

What?

Stage	Characteristics	Decision-making
Competent	- is able to "cope with crowdedness" (ability to multi-task) - deliberate planning - formulates routines	Rational
Proficient	- able to view issues holistically - prioritises importance of areas of work - ability to perceive deviations from usual patterns	Rational
Expert	- able to work flexibly relying on own judgement and tacit understanding - uses analytical approaches	Intuitive

Integrated developmental model

Developed by Stoltenberg, McNeill and Delworth (1998) this model identifies three over-riding structures:

- Self (and other) awareness
- Motivation
- Autonomy

Alongside eight specific domains of competence:

- Intervention skills
- Assessment technique
- Interpersonal assessment
- Client conceptualisation

- Individual differences
- Theoretical orientation
- Plans and goals
- Professional ethics

What?

The model identifies three developmental levels which are sometimes likened to human development stages:

Level 1
(likened to childhood)

Level 2
(likened to adolescence)

Level 3
(likened to maturity)

The model can be summarised as follows:

	Level 1	Level 2	Level 3
Self awareness	• limited self awareness • very self focussed • experiences difficulties in self-evaluation	• focus moves towards service user	• self aware • shows understanding of strengths and limitations
Motivation	• highly motivated • highly anxious	• fluctuates: sometimes highly motivated but increased complexity can cause confusion and create despair	• stable motivation secure in own professional identity

What?

	Level 1	**Level 2**	**Level 3**
Autonomy	• dependent on supervisor	• dependency versus autonomy conflict: can function independently but at other times dependent on supervisor	• autonomous recognising when consultation is required
Skills	• focus is on basic skills • seeks a 'right way' using a "cookbook" approach, looking for recipes for practice	• skill acquisition begins to recognise diversity and flexibility	• highly skilled with secure ethical framework

Integrated model of supervision (4x4x4)

Developed by Tony Morrison (2005), this model is sometimes referred to as the 4x4x4 model of supervision.

The model integrates the four functions of supervision:

- Managerial
- Developmental
- Mediation
- Supportive

With the four stages of the experimental learning cycle:

- Experience
- Reflection
- Analysis
- Planning

Whilst also recognising the four stakeholders:

- Service users
- Staff
- Organisation
- Partners

What?

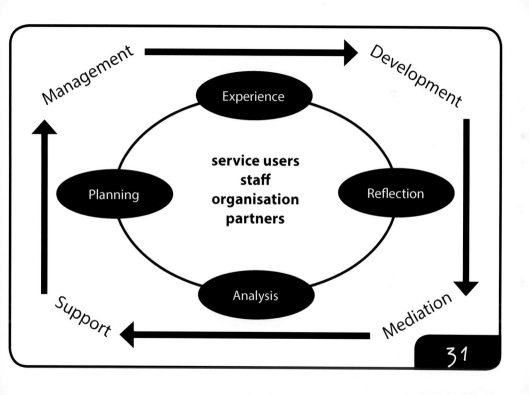

31

Interpersonal models

Interpersonal models of supervision focus on two main aspects:

Skills

Relationships

Much of the focus is on the use of interpersonal skills to nurture the supervisory relationship which will in turn improve the supervision process.

Shulman (1993) highlights that supervisors use the following specific skills to develop relationships in supervision:

- Sessional tuning-in skills
- Sessional contracting skills
- Elaborating skills
- Empathic skills
- Skills in sharing feelings

- Skills in making a demand for work
- Skills in pointing out obstacles
- Skills in sharing data
- Sessional ending skills

What?

Based on these skills, supervision becomes the practice of developing effective interactions and a functional relationship. Potter and Brittain (2009: 29) state *"A strong supervisor-worker relationship leads to a healthy supervisory experience: conversely, a negative or strained relationship will impinge on the integrity of the process."*

Indeed Ramos-Sanchez et al (2002) relate that the relationship between supervisor and supervisee is one of the most influential factors in supervisee satisfaction.

Some interpersonal models refer to the importance of wider relationships to effective supervision. For example, Tsui (2005) refers to relationships between the supervisor, supervisee, agency and service user with these relationships embedded in the supervisory process.

Interpersonal models also highlight the way that supervisors can draw on their professional knowledge, skills and experience filtered through their own reflective processes to facilitate the supervisee's learning and development.

Pflieger (2011) highlights the following eight characteristics that define relationships based aspects to reflective supervision.

1. Safety and trust

2. Mutuality of shared goals

3. Commitment to evolving growth and change

4. Commitment to reflecting on the work

5. Respect for and getting to know each other

6. Supervisor being sensitive to the content of the work environment

7. Open communication

8. Standards and ideals for staff to strive towards

Four As

Powell and Brodsky (1998) refer to the four As of the 'Good Supervisor' which can improve the supervisory relationship.

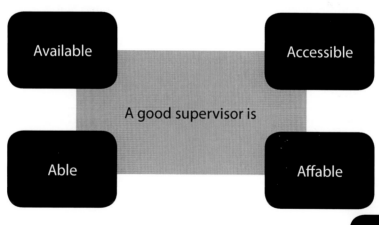

Available

Accessible

A good supervisor is

Able

Affable

35

Solution focussed supervision

Solution focussed approaches are developed from brief solution focussed therapy which grew out of the work of Steve de Shazer (1985) and his colleagues at the Brief Family Therapy Centre in the United States. Solution focussed approaches were quickly adopted in counselling and therapeutic work and many of the components of the approach are now utilised in social work practice. The way that solution focussed therapy has been adopted into solution focussed supervision can be summarised as follows (adapted from Waskett 2006):

Solution focussed therapy	Solution focussed supervision
Seeks to be helpful to the service user in their agenda.	Seeks to be helpful to the practitioner in their agenda for practice.
Focuses on solutions rather than problems.	Focuses on helping the worker find their own solutions.

What?

Solution focussed therapy	Solution focussed supervision
Uses a range of questioning techniques to help the service user identify their strengths and find their own solutions.	Uses a range of questionning to support the worker to develop a critically reflective approach.
Maintains professional boundaries - striving for best therapeutic practice.	Maintains professional boundaries as well as appropriate accountability.

According to Waskett (2006: 9) solution focussed supervision:

- Elicits the practitioner's strengths and resources
- Develops the supervisee's preferred outcome
- Takes a 'not-knowing position'
- Uses a range of appropriate questions
- Notes positive movements in small steps
- Offers appropriate evidence based feedback
- Stays curious, respectful and interested

This section has introduced the basic knowledge around supervision in social work. The 'how?' section seeks to support readers to consider how this knowledge can be used to improve supervisory practice.

It is vital to remember that effective supervision is a two-way process which needs the engagement, participation and commitment of everyone involved.

What?

WHY?

According to Henry (2010) "we all understand the importance of supervision", so this section of the Pocket Guide could potentially be very short if we simply considered why supervision is important in social work practice. However, Henry (2010) also recognises that there are a number of barriers to the provision of effective supervision, so this section will also explore the nature of these barriers.

So, in considering:

- Why is supervision important in social work practice?
- Why do social work supervisors struggle to provide good quality supervision?

This section should help you consider the central role of supervision to good social work practice.

WHY IS SUPERVISION SO IMPORTANT?

Why is supervision important to social work practice?

Good quality supervision:

Leads to improved outcomes for service users

Prevents burnout

Improves social work practice

Promotes a positive organisational culture and climate

Why?

Provides a 'fresh pair of eyes' when considering case work

Supports the development of analytical, critical and reflective thinking

Is the key factor in the recruitment and retention of social work practitioners

Enables social workers to develop their emotional intelligence

Improves decision making

41

Improving practice

Good quality supervision can help to improve social work practice on a range of levels. It supports a practitioner to reflect *on* their practice and to reflect *for* their future practice. This critical reflection will enable a practitioner to continually develop and improve their practice.

Research by the American National Association of Social Workers (Social Work Policy Institute 2011) identified that supervision rated as one of the top three factors impacting on job efficacy (the other two were caseload size and manageable paperwork - so no surprise there!)

The professional capabilities framework for social work recently introduced in England, recognises the vital importance of social workers making effective use of supervision to improve their practice.

Why?

There is growing evidence that the development of evidence based practice and cultural competence, specifically, are enhanced by supervision (Social Work Policy Institute 2011). Other aspects of work which can be improved by good quality supervision include:

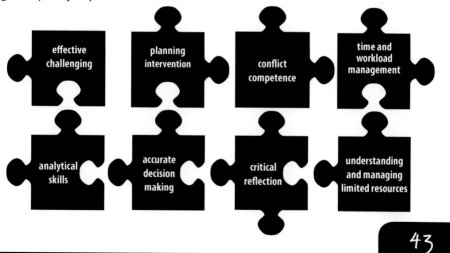

effective challenging

planning intervention

conflict competence

time and workload management

analytical skills

accurate decision making

critical reflection

understanding and managing limited resources

43

Improved outcomes for service users

The Social Work Reform Board (2011 online) asserts that *"Good supervision has been shown to provide more consistent outcomes for children, adults and families."* Further, the Childrens Workforce Development Council and Skills for Care (2007) claim that supervision *"should optimise the capacity of people who use services to lead independent and fulfilling lives."*

Certainly, it is commonly accepted that effective supervision leads to improved outcomes for service users (eg: see Morrison 2005). The actual evidence about the impact of supervision on service users is, however, quite limited. See for example Harkness and Hensley (1991) and Wonnacott (2003). To some extent, it could be seen as an assumption that supervision leads to more effective outcomes for service users (although most practitioners would say a fair assumption).

Why?

Morrison (2005: 20) makes clear that supervision only improves outcomes for service users if certain conditions are met. These conditions include:

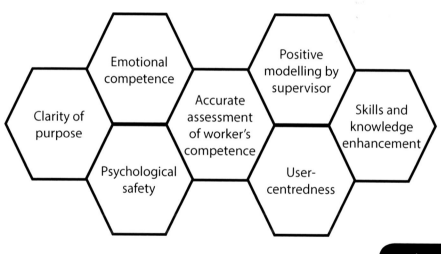

Emotional competence

Positive modelling by supervisor

Clarity of purpose

Accurate assessment of worker's competence

Skills and knowledge enhancement

Psychological safety

User-centredness

Improving decision making

Stevenson (2005) claims that the element of supervision which social workers value most is the concept of shared decision making. According to Stevenson, shared decision making involves six main safeguards and benefits:

1. Peer review of professional decisions
2. Protection of civil liberties: ensuring that no service user's liberty is affected without scrutiny of that decision
3. Protection of service users: service users are not left in unacceptable risks on the basis of an individual's assessment or actions
4. Protection of staff: ensuring that professionals are not put in positions where situations may exceed their knowledge, skills or experience or where they have to deal with very stressful situations

Why?

5. Protection of the agency: shared decision making ensures a fail safe element and confirms that the agency has taken the importance of scrutiny seriously

6. It encourages openness and collective responsibility and creates a climate where professionals are open about their decision and can explore the reasons for this. A culture should be created where practitioners are prepared to jointly take responsibility for key decisions and to achieve this are prepared to challenge each other in the interests of the service user and indeed the agency.

(Stevenson 2005)

Shared decision making in supervision ensures more defensible decision making and enhances a practitioner's ability to develop more autonomous practice whilst recognising the need for accountability.

Emotional intelligence

Emotional intelligence (sometimes referred to as EI) is widely referred to in leadership and management, and the concept of the emotionally intelligent workplace is growing in popularity. Cherniss and Goleman (2001) argue that if you *"look deeply at almost any factor that influences organisational effectiveness, you will find that emotional intelligence plays a part."*

The importance of social workers being emotionally intelligent is now widely recognised. For example, Howe (2008) describes social work as *"emotional work of a high order."* He goes on to highlight the fact that the more emotionally intelligent social workers are, the more sensitive, thoughtful and effective their practice will be. Hennessey (2011) argues that emotional intelligence supports social workers to develop sound 'multi-dimensional practice'.

Why?

Emotional intelligence is about practitioners recognising emotions in themselves and others. Using this recognition helps practitioners to connect, engage and build relationships. Emotional intelligence promotes collaboration and reduces the negative impact of conflict. It also aids thinking and perceptions and supports the management of emotions - thus promoting professional resilience.

Reflective supervision can support social workers to become more emotionally aware and can enhance practitioners emotional intelligence. Research by Grant and Kinman (2009) highlights the importance of emotional intelligence and reflective ability in social work practice. These two aspects are highlighted as key characteristics of social workers "who fly".

Organisational culture and climate

Organisational culture has a significant impact on the provision of supervision and good quality supervision can have a very positive impact on organisational culture. Where good quality supervision permeates an organisation, the organisation is likely to become more reflective and more responsive to the needs of service users.

good quality supervision

positive organisational culture

Why?

In England part of the social work reform programme involves employers carrying out "health checks" on social work services. The idea of this is to ensure that practitioners can operate safely and that effective social work environments are provided. Recognising the close two-way links between organisational culture and supervision, a key aspect of the health checks focuses on the quality of supervision provided.

Prevention of burnout

Kadushin (1992) recognised that supervision needs to provide a forum to remove a worker from the stress of their work and provide an opportunity for discussion about stress and the strategies for managing this. In fact, there is a widespread recognition that supervision is one of the main defenses against burnout and compassion fatigue in social work practice (see, for example, ANAS 2010 and the International Federation of Social Workers 2010).

The Charter of Rights for Social Workers issued by the International Federation of Social Workers, European Region (2011) highlights that practitioners have a right to good quality supervision in order to avoid burnout.

> One of the requirements in the social work role is to stay close to, and empathetic with, people at times of stress and pain. At times, all of this can be overwhelming... Supervision should provide a safe and secure space for these stresses and strains to be shared with the supervisor, as well as reflected and acted upon.
>
> Jones (2011: 1

Why?

Recruitment and retention

Research (for example, Livingstone 2000, Eborall and Garmeson 2001, Manchester City Council 2010) highlights that:

- Good quality supervision is one of the key factors in recruitment to social care and social work: Effectively, it is the most important 'selling point' an employer has.

- Where practitioners feel they receive good quality supervision, they are likely to remain in post significantly longer.

- Social workers who are satisfied with the quality of their supervision are likely to remain in 'front line' practice for longer. This is a key point for employers who can struggle to recruit and retain the most experienced practitioners.

Why do supervisors struggle to provide good quality supervision?

The benefits of supervision do not come simply from the provision of any type of supervision. Regular, good quality, supervision is required. Despite this, many supervisors struggle to provide what practitioners consider to be 'good quality' supervision. The reasons for this are varied, but might include:

Pressures of time and workload

Climate of contemporary practice

Lack of professional understanding

Why?

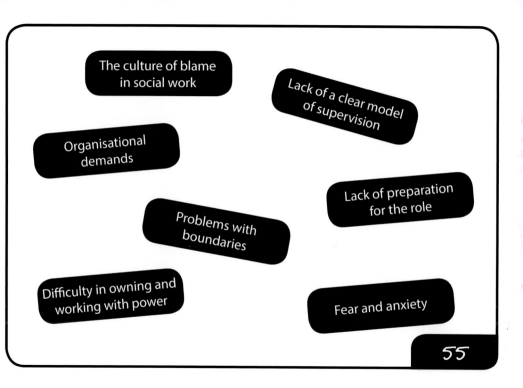

The culture of blame in social work

Lack of a clear model of supervision

Organisational demands

Lack of preparation for the role

Problems with boundaries

Difficulty in owning and working with power

Fear and anxiety

55

The 'Supervisor Squeeze'

Supervisors often talk of feeling pulled in different directions. Dewane coined the visual term "supervisor squeeze". This refers to the fact that supervision is generally provided by middle managers who are *"caught in the squeeze of trying to help workers and service users whilst also meeting agency demands."* (Dewane 2007: 34)

Why?

Walking the tightrope

Social work supervisors are often under immense stress and as the concept of the supervisor squeeze demonstrates, they may feel their role acting effectively as a bridge between practitioners and the organisation is untenable.

Certainly, balancing the functions of supervision in this context can be particularly difficult. Bogo and Dill (2008) describe it like trying 'to walk a tightrope'.

Preparation for the role

Many commentators (eg: see Munson 2002, Dewane 2007, Social Work Policy Institute 2011) have pointed out that very often social workers who are given responsibility for supervising others are not effectively prepared for the role. Historically, there has been little training in supervision skills. There appears to be a working assumption that because someone has been supervised, they will know how to supervise others. How ridiculous this seems if we apply the thinking to other areas - would we say that because someone has received social work services, they will know how to be a good social worker?

Thankfully, supervision training now appears to be on the professional agenda. In England, the Social Work Reform Board (2010) recommended that employers should *"provide regular supervision training for social work supervisors."* It remains to be seen, however, whether practitioners moving into a supervisory role, will receive effective preparation and training.

Why?

Lack of a clear model of supervision

As the 'What?' section demonstrated, social work draws on various models of supervision. The general lack of research into what works in supervision means no model has a clear universally agreed evidence base. Supervision in social work could therefore be likened to a doughnut - it has a hole in the middle. This can lead to supervisors being uncertain about how best to go about providing supervision.

Contemporary practice

Much has been written about the challenges of contemporary practice, the focus on performance measures, an extreme lack of resources and high workloads. The impact of this contemporary environment on supervision was illustrated most strongly for me when a colleague of mine recently told me that she has to ask two set questions at the beginning of each supervision session - *"How much have you 'spent' this month?"* and *"How much have you saved the department?"*

As the social work landscape has to contend with a more conservative and fiscally restrictive environment, so too has practice supervision become more focussed on efficiency, accountability and worker performance often at the expense of professional and practice development. In addition, current research has identified a crisis in the probity of practice supervision where many practitioners cite disillusionment and despair, as well as lack of opportunity to stop and critically reflect on practice situations as another challenge in this changed climate.

(Noble and Irwin 2009)

Why?

Culture of blame

Social work operates in a difficult culture. The culture of blame is widely recognised and social workers often feel they are "damned if they do and damned if they don't." Essentially, this culture can lead to supervision focussing simply on the managerial function at the expense of holistic good quality supervision.

The focal point for supervision can tend to be a response to the culture of blame by examining workers procedural decisions.

(Davies and Leonard 2004: 53)

Difficulty in owning and working with power

Despite the fact that social work is essentially about power many practitioners are uncomfortable about power.

In any relationship between two people, there are power dynamics which can impact on the way that the relationship functions. Of course, all of the usual issues around societal power will impact on the supervisory relationship (for example, differences between the supervisee and supervisor in terms of age, gender, class etc).

Added to this, supervision in itself creates an unequal role relationship with the supervisor occupying an authority role which is intrinsically more powerful. The Inner London Probation Service (1993) identify the following sources of power in the supervisory relationship:

Why?

Professional / expert power

The supervisor has professional power so they will be viewed as the 'expert' in the relationship.

Resource power

Supervisors are likely to have more power over resources - this may or may not include budgetary power.

The power to determine

This is often the source of power which is most acute in the supervisee's mind. For example, the supervisor is likely to have the power to determine issues such as whether a practitioner is deemed as capable or competent, when they can take leave, what their working pattern is, what work they undertake etc.

63

Professional understanding

In recent years there has been an increased emphasis on collaborative working and moves towards integrated or multi-disciplinary teams, not only in the United Kingdom but on a Global basis. This has had a significant impact on social work supervision with an increasing number of social workers finding themselves being supervised by a person who does not hold a social work qualification. Berger and Mizrahi (2001) refer to this as *"non-social work supervision".*

Where the supervisor and supervisee are from different professional backgrounds this can create difficulties, particularly in terms of the clarity of professional understanding.

O'Donoghue (2012) claims that clear guidelines are essential if cross-disciplinary supervision is to be effective. The following guidelines are adapted from his suggestions:

Why?

- The similarity and differences between each profession's supervision traditions are discussed

- Both parties are informed about each other's ethical codes and complaints procedures

- The status of the supervision in relation to regulatory, professional membership, and organisational requirements is clear and explicit

O'Donoghue (2012: 8) also makes clear that cross-disciplinary supervision should be in addition to 'professional supervision with a social worker'.

This section has demonstrated that there are many reasons why good quality supervision is important to social work practice. Improving the professional capability and confidence of social workers is essential and effective supervision is one of the most effective ways of doing this. Cohan and Laufer (1999) clearly identified that social workers who are satisfied with their supervision have stronger perceptions of their own professional competence and are more prepared for autonomous practice. Therefore, supervisors who provide good quality supervision are likely to find that their commitment is paid off in terms of longer term time management.

The next section provides some practical guidance on how to improve supervision practice.

Why?

HOW?

This section provides a range of practical tips for the provision of effective supervision, building on the 'What?' and 'Why?' sections of the Pocket Guide.

These tips could be used by a variety of practitioners who may be involved in supporting other practitioners in a range of ways - for example, those acting as 'mentors' or 'buddies' and those taking on a supervisory role in practice learning.

Recognising that supervision is *"not done by the supervisor but rather jointly by the supervisor and supervisee together"* (Hawkins 2008: 3), this section will also be useful for practitioners seeking to make the most of the supervision they receive.

HOW DO I PROVIDE EFFECTIVE SUPERVISION?

How do I improve supervision?

A variety of steps can be taken to improve supervision practice. The following practical hints, which are covered in more detail in the remainder of this Guide, can be particularly useful:

Create a positive environment

Listen effectively

Use the experiential learning cycle

Reflect on your own experiences of supervision and draw from the positives

Start from the functions of supervision to develop an effective strategy

Develop an effective supervision agreement

How?

Maintain a focus on the quality of outcomes for service users

Respond to individual learning styles

Record supervision effectively

Provide constructive feedback

Maintain the balance with performance management

Promote reflection

Encourage hopeful social work practice

Be creative in your use of questions

Create a positive environment

The environment in which people practice and learn is recognised as vital and you will have often heard the term "a safe learning environment". It is important to work to provide a 'safe supervision environment'. It can be useful to draw on adult learning theory to inform the management of the supervision environment. Billington (1996) identified seven characteristics of effective environments for adult learning:

1. Ensuring people feel safe and supported, where individual needs and uniqueness are acknowledged and respected.
2. Fostering intellectual freedom and encouraging experimentation and creativity.
3. Accepting and respecting opinions.
4. Encouraging people to take responsibility for their own practice and learning.

How?

5. Ensuring pacing or intellectual challenge: optimal pacing is challenging people just beyond their present level of ability. If challenged too little or too much, people lose motivation.

6. Active involvement and partnership in creating the environment.

7. Regular two-way feedback mechanisms.

In seeking to evaluate their supervisory practice, supervisors could consider to what extent they ensure these seven characteristics are present in the supervision they provide.

Don't forget some of the real basics about the supervision environment - is the room private? Is it sufficiently warm / cool? Are the chairs comfortable? etc..........

Draw on the positives

Munson (2002) claims that supervisors draw on their own experiences of receiving supervision as the major influence on how they provide supervision. It is therefore important that social workers taking on the responsibility for supervising others reflect on their own experiences of supervision.

In my work with practice educators and social work managers I ask them to begin by reflecting on their own experiences of supervision, considering what has made supervision a positive experience for them, and what has made supervision a negative experience. What they have shared with me is recorded across the next few pages. One of the issues that has particularly interested me in carrying out this exercise over a number of years is that people generally agree on what makes supervision a negative experience for them. However, there is not always such a clear agreement about what makes supervision positive. Indeed, what makes supervision a positive experience for one person might make it a negative experience for another person.

How?

This is confirmed by Magnuson, Norem and Wilcoxon (2000) who relate that there is generally significant agreement about what constitutes 'bad' supervision, but much less clarity about what constitutes 'good' supervision within the profession generally.

Understanding what makes supervision a positive or negative experience can be a useful starting point. It is therefore always worth a supervisor starting a supervisory relationship by asking the supervisee what makes supervision a positive or negative experience for them. Morrison (2005) refers to this as taking a 'supervision history.'

Clearly in order to provide effective supervision the supervisor and supervisee should seek to ensure that they avoid the characteristics of negative supervision and promote those of positive supervision.

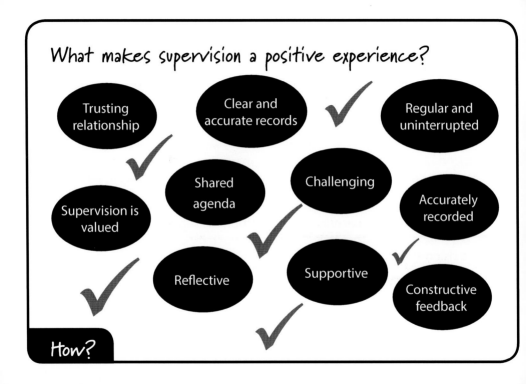

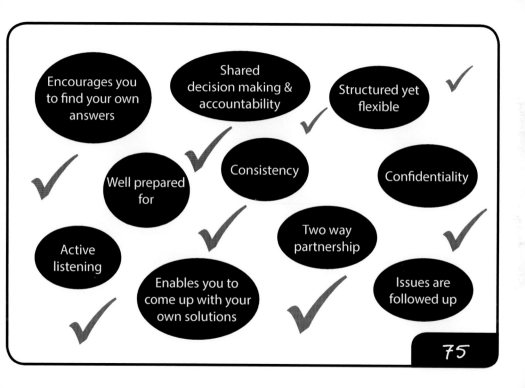

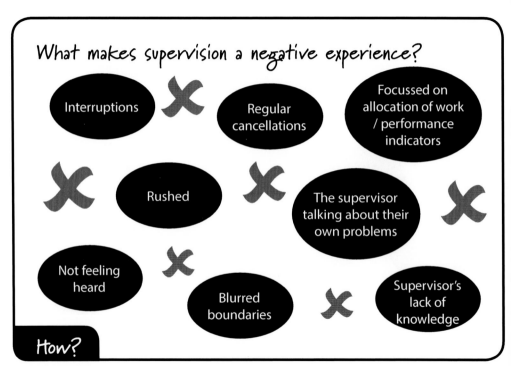

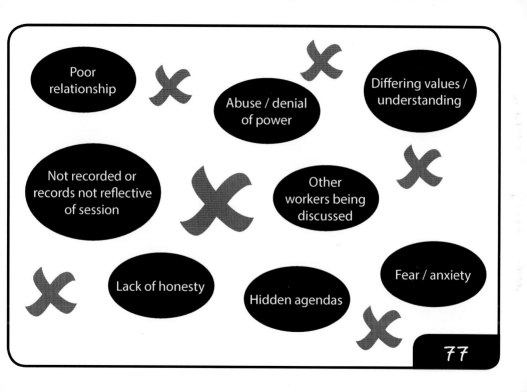

Work from the functions of supervision

When providing supervision, it is important to plan a strategy which has the needs of a practitioner to receive all four "functions" of supervision at its heart.

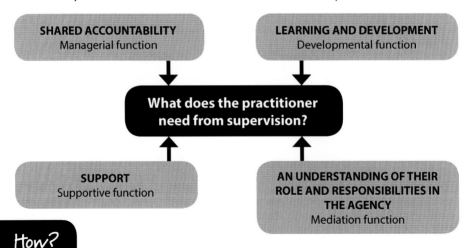

SHARED ACCOUNTABILITY
Managerial function

LEARNING AND DEVELOPMENT
Developmental function

What does the practitioner need from supervision?

SUPPORT
Supportive function

AN UNDERSTANDING OF THEIR ROLE AND RESPONSIBILITIES IN THE AGENCY
Mediation function

How?

Supervisors who try to address all four functions of supervision in each supervision session are likely to find it very difficult to keep all "the plates spinning" and may well find that the balance between the functions is lost.

Working from the individual practitioner's needs and the four functions of supervision means that responsibility for ensuring each of the functions of supervision can be shared. Different people providing different forms of supervision can work to ensure the supervisee receives everything they need in order to practice effectively.

How?

The following examples provide some ideas of how a practitioner / functions centred strategy can work:

- A newly qualified practitioner receives managerial supervision from the team manager. This focuses predominantly on the managerial function whilst also providing for the mediation function. They also receive developmental supervision sessions with a senior practitioner within the team. This focuses on the developmental and supportive functions.

  To ensure that everyone receives what they need from supervision involve other people and use the variety of forms of supervision.

- A team manager recognises that time constraints means the supervision she provides mostly focuses on managerial / administrative issues. She organises a monthly peer group supervision session which focuses more on reflection, to ensure that the developmental function is also addressed for team members.

- A team manager feels that providing informal supervision is taking a disproportionate amount of her time - she therefore arranges a buddy system in the team so that practitioners can consult with each other.

Focus on outcomes for service users

Harkness and Hensley (1991) reported a significant degree of enhanced client satisfaction from those social workers who had received supervision which focussed on improving service user outcomes.

In seeking to be outcomes focussed in practice, sometimes supervisors concentrate on more easily measured performance indicators - such as whether requirements for the completion of documentation have been met. In fact, Bowers, Esmond and Canales (1999) clearly identified that supervisors tend to focus much more on the filling in of forms rather than on the quality of outcomes for service users.

As a supervisor, reflect on the ways that you can maintain a user-focussed approach to supervision. Some of the following ideas may help:

How?

Ensure that both you and the supervisee recognise that supervision is about ensuring and enhancing the quality of practice that service users experience

Ask the supervisee user focussed questions, for example "How might the service user feel about that?"

Draw on feedback from service users (both formal and informal) in supervision discussion

Discuss service user's goals in supervision

Use supervision to critically reflect on the outcomes of practice for service users

Discuss any observations you have made of the supervisee's practice - reflecting on the service user's experiences

Supervision agreements

Most agencies have standard supervision agreements. It is important though that the development of a supervision agreement involves more than the supervisor and supervisee simply reading the agreement form and signing it. The discussion that takes place when the agreement is being developed is, in many ways, more important than the actual agreement (the document).

Morrison (2005) suggests a four stage approach to negotiating an agreement:

Clarifying the mandate

This stage involves agreeing the basis of supervision - what is negotiable and non-negotiable? What responsibilities does each person have? What are the agency requirements? What is the agreed definition of supervision?

Engagement

This stage is about discussing previous experiences of supervision, how authority will be handled, values and attitudes, how emotions are expressed and how supervision can be supportive.

How?

Acknowledging Ambivilance

This is about exploring what could present barriers or blocks to effective supervision and how these should be managed. Anticipating where conflict may occur and how this can be pro-actively addressed is vital. One of the main areas to be considered here is how strong emotional responses to work can be managed. Supervisees need to know that it is OK to not always feel competent and in control, and that supervision will provide a safe forum to discuss this.

Written contract

Only when the first three stages have been addressed should the agreement be put into writing. It is important that each supervision agreement is unique to the individual. Morrisson (2005) suggests that agreements should:

- be arrived at through negotiation
- address issues and how they will be managed
- be signed by both parties and shared
- be reviewed at least annually

85

Use the experiential learning cycle

Experiential learning is sometimes misinterpreted as simply being about the fact that people learn from experience. To some extent this is true, but experiential learning theory asserts that it's not enough for people to have an experience - they won't learn from this unless they spend time reflecting on the experience, making wider links and drawing conclusions.

Perhaps the most well known academic to write about experiential learning is Kolb (1984). He describes a cycle of experiential learning. The stages of this cycle are referred to in Morrison's integrated model of supervision (see pages 30-31).

Good quality supervision will support a practitioner to move through the experiential learning cycle - reflecting on their practice, making links and drawing conclusions to plan future action.

How?

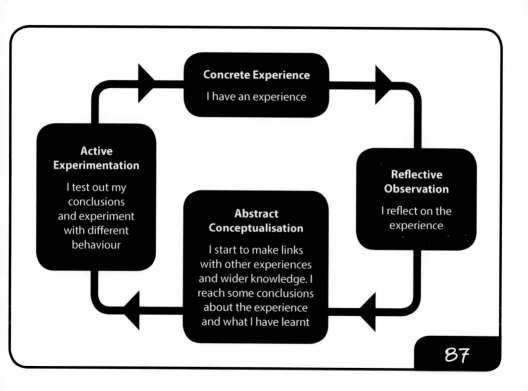

Concrete Experience

I have an experience

Active Experimentation

I test out my conclusions and experiment with different behaviour

Abstract Conceptualisation

I start to make links with other experiences and wider knowledge. I reach some conclusions about the experience and what I have learnt

Reflective Observation

I reflect on the experience

87

You can use Kolb's cycle in a range of ways in the supervisory process:

Developing a 'coaching conversation'
Practitioners need to be supported to move round the full cycle in order to learn from their experiences and to develop their practice. It can be useful to 'coach' the worker round the cycle by developing a coaching conversation as illustrated in the following diagram. Supporting practitioners around the cycle will also assist in promoting more effective decision making - since concluding and planning are the final part of the cycle.

Recognising 'blocks'
As a supervisor, you may find that practitioners get 'stuck' at certain parts of the cycle. For example, a practitioner may be able to reflect and perhaps draw conclusions about what they would do differently next time, but then they appear to repeat mistakes. They may be getting stuck at the active experimentation stage. Here you will be able to make use of the coaching conversation and concentrate supervision questionning and discussion in this area.

How?

Experience
DOING

Encourage the practitioner to outline the situation and their work or plan briefly.

Experimentation
PLANNING

Help the practitioner to plan how to implement their learning eg: How will you put that into practice?

Think widely about your use of questions in supervision and use the whole of this section to support you in constructing questions to take people through the whole cycle of learning

Reflection
THINKING

Ask questions to encourage personal reflection - eg: How do you feel about that?

Conceptualisation
CONCLUDING

Support the practitioner to make wider links and draw conclusions eg: What conclusions can you draw?

Respond to individual learning styles

Honey and Mumford (1982) report that people have different styles of learning. They developed four different styles, and designed a questionnaire which identifies which style a person prefers (often referred to as a learning styles questionnaire or a learning styles inventory).

The four styles identified by Honey and Mumford are:

Activists **Pragmatists** **Theorists** **Reflectors**

The styles can be linked closely with Kolb's learning cycle and an understanding of the way that learning styles and the learning cycle link can be helpful in planning supervisory approaches for people with different learning styles.

How?

Activists

Activists tend to be open minded and enthusiastic. They like new experiences and want to get involved in the here and now. They enjoy "getting stuck in" to something and learn by doing. Activists can become bored when an activity stops and will want to quickly move onto the next challenge or activity rather than dwelling on the last activity.

If you are supervising an activist, it is important to value their energy and enthusiasm. You will however, need to ensure they reflect on their practice and consider the value of theory, evidence and other perspectives on practice.

Reflectors

Reflectors do just what it says on the tin! They stand back, reflect, ponder and consider many perspectives before acting. Reflectors need to mull things over to feel comfortable in reaching a conclusion. They observe, gather information and use plenty of time to think things over.

If you are supervising a reflector, make sure you value their thoughts and reflections. You will, however, need to ensure that they don't procrastinate and avoid action.

How?

Theorists

Theorists are logical thinkers. They analyse, question and learn, step by step, in a logical way. Theorists question any new learning and want to make sure that they fully understand the learning and that it fits and makes sense with their logical approach. Theorists are often perfectionists and don't appreciate flippant approaches to a subject.

If you are supervising a theorist, value their logical approach and encourage their analysis. You will however, need to ensure that they take the emotional context of work into account and that they translate their analysis into practical action.

Pragmatists

Pragmatists like to try new things out to see if they work in practice. They are essentially experimenters. They will often take a problem solving approach to learning and will seek to apply something that they have learnt straight away. However, if their "experiment" doesn't work they are unlikely to try the approach again – they will look for something else to try out instead.

If you are supervising a pragmatist, value their ideas and problem solving skills. You will, however, need to ensure that they don't take a corner cutting approach to systems and that they put policy and procedure into practice.

How?

Understanding your own style

Whilst it is useful to understand the learning style of the person you are supervising, it is also important to know and understand your own style and to recognise the impact that this might have on the way you provide supervision.

Think through:

- Do you have the same or a different learning style to the supervisee?

- What impact might this have on the supervision you provide? For example, if you share similar styles, could this lead to collusion and potentially avoiding some aspects of supervision? If you have different styles, could this lead to conflict or miscommunication?

Provide constructive feedback

What makes feedback constructive is not whether you are being told you did a job well or whether you did a job badly. The way the feedback is given is what makes it constructive (or not!)

The way that feedback is received will also have an impact on whether the feedback is constructive. Rich (2009) suggests that in receiving feedback, people take either a negative (closed) or positive (open) style. As a supervisor, you can support people to take a more 'open' style by providing a reflective environment, building trust and being open to feedback yourself.

The main elements of constructive / destructive feedback are summarised in the following table.

How?

Constructive Feedback	Destructive Feedback
Solves problems	Intensifies problems
Concentrates on behaviour / work performance	Concentrates on personality
Strengthens relationships	Damages relationships
Builds trust	Destroys trust
Is a two-way process	Is one-way
Reduces stress and tension	Adds to stress and increases tension
Manages conflict	Creates conflict
Helps development	Hinders development
Is assertive	Is aggressive

Constructive Feedback should be:

'Sandwiched': Feedback should always start and finish with a positive. This is often referred to as the positive sandwich. The 'content' of the sandwich should give the practitioner something to work on whilst the bread highlights the positive aspects of their practice which they can consolidate. Using this sandwich approach, the practitioner's esteem and motivation will be built on and they will be more 'open' to receive feedback.

Specific: Deal clearly with particular instances and behaviour rather than making vague or sweeping statements.

Actionable: Direct feedback towards behaviour that can be changed.

Balanced: The feedback should balance support and challenge effectively.

How?

Prioritised: Concentrate on the two or three key areas for improvement, preferably including those where the practitioner can see a quick return. Break down a major problem into smaller, step-by-step goals. (This is the 'content' of the positive sandwich).

Facilitative: Rather than prescribing behaviour, feedback should help the recipient question their behaviour and make them more reflective about where they are going wrong. For example, you could ask the practitioner "How might that have been interpreted by the service user?"

Well Timed: The most useful feedback is given when the person is receptive to it and it is sufficiently close to the event to be fresh in their mind.

Clear: Avoid jargon wherever possible and ensure that your communication is clear. Always check feedback to ensure that it is understood by the recipient.

Open: There should be no hidden messages in the feedback. Make sure that you are open and that you are able to offer suggestions about what could have been done differently.

Promote reflection

Current trends in policy are placing more emphasis on the role of reflective supervision in contemporary social work. Significant research is taking place into the role of "clinical" supervision and the emphasis on reflection within this (eg: Pack 2009) and there is a growing amount of literature to support supervisors in developing reflective supervision (eg: Scaife 2010). To promote reflective supervision, it is important to understand the different forms of reflection, as outlined by Schön (1983) and Killian and Todnem (1991).

Reflection *for* action	Reflection before undertaking the work
Reflection *in* action	Reflection when carrying out the work
Reflection *on* action	Reflection after undertaking the work

How?

These forms of reflection relate closely to Greenaway's (1995) basic framework for reflection.

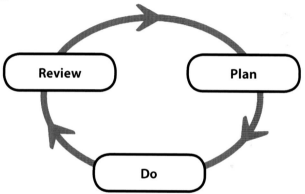

Whilst reflective supervision should support a practitioner to become more reflective *in* action, generally supervision provides an ideal opportunity to support a practitioner to plan (reflect *for*) and review (reflect *on*) their practice.

101

You can promote reflective supervision by:

- Drawing on specific models of critically reflective practice (see the Social Work Pocket Guide to Reflective Practice)
- Using reflective questionning
- Encouraging practitioners to explore the outcomes of their practice in depth
- Encouraging practitioners to develop their self awareness
- Exploring the impact of values and ethics on practice
- Encouraging practitioners to identify the evidence they are drawing on
- Supporting practitioners to understand what is impacting on their reflection
- Allowing some silence in supervision to promote reflection
- Where supervisees are completing learning programmes, they are likely to have to complete reflective accounts - make sure you discuss these in supervision

How?

Be a 'Critical Friend'

The concept of critical friendships was first introduced by Stenhouse (1975) as a method to support action research. The concept has more recently been developed as something which supports reflective practice. The idea of this is that the critical friend acts as an interested 'sounding board'. The critical friend listens to the practitioner and asks pro-active questions which promote deeper thinking and encourage the practitioner to reflect on their work.

"OH NO YOU REALLY DON'T LOOK GOOD IN THAT"

NOT THAT KIND OF CRITICAL FRIEND

Research into the use of critical friends in medical education indicates that whilst having a critical friend is useful, it might be even more advantageous for the person acting as the critical friend in terms of the development of reflective practice skills (Dahlgren et al 2006).

103

Reflective questionning

McClure (2002: 5-6) suggests that reflective practice is about a process of dynamic questioning and suggests that 'reflective questions' can be used to assist in developing critical reflection. The following adaptations of McClure's questions could be helpful to encourage more reflective supervision.

- What were you aiming for when you did that?
- What exactly did you do? (describing it precisely)
- Why did you choose that particular action?
- What theories/models/research informed your practice?
- What were you trying to achieve?
- What did you do next? Why?
- How successful was it?

How?

- What criteria are you using to judge success?

- What alternatives were there?

- Could you have dealt with the situation any better?

- How would you do it differently next time?

- What do you feel about the whole experience?

- What knowledge/ values/ skills did you use?

- How did the service user feel about it?

- How do you know the service user felt like that?

- What sense can you make of this in the light of your past experience?

- Has this changed the way in which you will do things in the future?

105

Creative use of questionning

Very often, supervisors ask questions which focus on the service user's 'story'. Whilst it is important for a supervisor to be aware of the outcomes for service users and to demonstrate a user centred approach, questions which focus on the service user's story / experiences will not enable the practitioner to critically reflect on their practice. To open up the questions asked in supervision, it can be useful to use a range of GEMS questions drawn out of solution focussed therapy (de Shazer 1985):

G - Goal setting questions

E - Exception finding questions

M - Miracle questions

S - Scaling questions

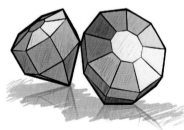

How?

Goal setting questions

Goal setting questions are designed to assist the practitioner to identify the goals for their intervention. Goal setting questions might encourage the practitioner to think about their goals or those of the service user.

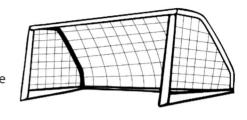

How will you know when your goals have been achieved?

What is the service user hoping to get out of your intervention?

What are you hoping to achieve?

What outcomes are you looking for?

Exception finding questions

These are questions that support the practitioner to identify the successful strategies they have used in the past. The intention is to help the practitioner to move away from a problem focussed narrative to a recognition of their capabilities. These questions will support the practitioner to see what resources and strengths they have and will give the practitioner the confidence to apply their own strategies to resolve what they see as impossible situations.

You say you've no idea what to do. When you've faced 'no solution' situations before, what have you done?

You're very skilled at developing intervention plans. How might you draw on these skills now?

How?

Miracle questions

Widely used in social work practice, miracle questions can help practitioners identify how their intervention and practice could be different. The most common miracle questions like *"If you had a magic wand, what would you do with it?"* or *"if you had three wishes to use on this case, what would they be?"* could be useful to help the practitioner look differently at the situation, although they are likely to simply lead to responses about the need for more resources or easier access to services. More creative miracle questionning can really prompt deeper thinking and more creative practice.

- If you had a time machine and could go back to any stage of this person's life, at what point would you have intervened? Why?

- If you could design a machine to do everything that would be needed in this situation, what would it look like and what would it do?

Scaling questions

Scaling questions are often used in risk assessment and in assessing eligibility for services etc. Scaling questions can be helpful in a range of ways in supervision. For example,

> On a scale of 1 to 10, how responsible do you feel for what happened?

> You said you're unsure about that. On a scale of 1 to 10, how confident are you?

Within supervision, it can be particularly useful to think about following up scaling questions with 'tailed' questions, such as "You say you are on a 4: What would it take to make you feel more like 8 or 9?"

How?

Listen effectively

Everyone involved in social work practice knows the vital importance of active listening, so this advice for supervisors risks being patronising. It is however, essential to point out the importance of truly effective listening in supervision. A wide range of issues can impact on the quality of listening in supervision. Rushton and Nathan (1996) quote a manager as saying:

Effective listening, reflective phrasing and paraphrasing are key social work skills which are also important in demonstrating active listening and valuing the practitioner in supervision. After you next provide supervision, reflect on how well you 'listened' to the supervisee. It's such a basic skill that it is often forgotten!

> If they tell you what they're feeling, what the hell can I do about it? Maybe some of my holding back (from the staff member) is because I think if they tell me all this, what can I do except say, well, you've got to carry on. Hold on."

Encourage 'Hopeful Practice'

Practitioners in mental health will be familiar with the recovery model. This model recognises the vital importance of people retaining a sense of hope to promote wellbeing and refers to the importance of people having someone who will hold a 'candle of hope'. People who achieve 'recovery' relate the importance of having people around them who continue to hope and convey a sense of confidence that 'recovery' will occur.

The concept of 'hopeful social work practice' has developed out of this in Australia. Stanford (2011) asserts that hopeful social work practice can assist social workers struggling in the contemporary social work climate to maintain their professional focus and values in day to day practice.

How?

Social workers may develop cynical approaches and may be resistant to, and negative about, change. This can be challenging for supervisors particularly in addressing the mediation function of supervision. Drawing on the concept of hopeful practice could be useful in this respect.

Miller and Powers (1988: 8) see hopeful social work as a multi-dimensional construct drawing on crucial elements of hope. Some of these may be useful to promote in social work supervision. Ensure that supervision provides the practitioner with a sense that:

✓ They "belong" (to a community of practice).
✓ Things are possible.
✓ They are achieving goals.
✓ Even small achievements are valued and important (every journey begins with a single step).
✓ There are a range of solutions.
✓ Every difficulty provides an opportunity.

Draw on a range of models

As discussed on page 59 there is no singularly accepted model of supervision in social work - leaving a hole in the middle (the doughnut). Personally, I've always preferred jam doughnuts. Drawing on a variety of the models of supervision as covered in the 'What?' section of this pocket guide; theorising from these and developing a personal model of supervision can go some way to providing the jam.

Draw on the range of models of supervision and develop something that works for you to fill the doughnut

How?

Avoid snoopervision

Kaduskin and Harkness (2002) refer to the concept of 'Snoopervision' where the purpose and nature of professional supervision has been misunderstood, perhaps on the basis of a misunderstanding of the concept.

Supervision must be about more than simply 'overseeing' performance if it is to have any value.

Recording supervision

Many organisations provide a pro-forma for the recording of supervision. This can mean that only minimal thought goes into what is recorded and the recording may well focus on managerial issues.

In considering how supervision should be recorded, it's important to establish what information pertains to:

The practitioner

Service users

How?

Information about service users

Discussion about cases, and particularly the influence of these discussions on decisions, should be recorded in case files for legal reasons. Any shared decisions or supervisor direction should be easily located as this should be available for court processes, audit purposes and complaints investigations.

It is also important for new workers and agency staff to be able to see what decisions have been made so that they can pick up on what action is still required.

Agencies should have clear requirements about the recording of information which relates to service users - this should cover how the issues are recorded, where the notes are kept etc. Make sure that both you and the supervisee are familiar with these requirements and that you record all information relating to service users in line with these requirements.

Information about the practitioner

In addressing all the functions of supervision, a number of issues will arise that relate predominantly to the practitioner and their experiences as opposed to any specific service user. This could relate to:

- The practitioner's needs for support
- The practitioner's progress against any learning / development needs
- The practitioner's ongoing learning and development needs
- Any concerns about practice or capability
- The practitioner's thoughts about supervision
- The practitioner's reflections, particularly any specific concerns they have

To promote candid reflection, supervisees need to be clear about where this information will be recorded and how it will be stored.

How?

Methods of recording

Increasingly, supervision is recorded electronically. Supervisors will need to be aware of the way that this can create barriers to the supervisory relationship - even with regard to demonstrating active listening. If the supervisor is concentrating on typing and looking at a computer screen, this will have an impact on the supervisee's feelings of being listened to and being valued and therefore their satisfaction with the supervision experience.

Agency requirements for recording should be discussed with the supervisee and agreed as part of the agreement negotiations. It might be worth considering sharing responsibilities for recording - for example, the supervisor might record the information which relates to service users, whilst the supervisee might record the information which relates to them.

It is important to be clear that supervisees should have a copy of any records which relate to them. Since practitioners may make use of these in a range of ways - eg: to demonstrate their professional capability or their development, these should not contain any information which can identify service users.

Performance Management

Supervision is an important part of the performance management cycle and performance management is an important part of supervision. However, it is vitally important to remember that performance management isn't just about supervision and supervision isn't just about performance management. The following diagram demonstrates how the two overlap but also have unique aspects.

Performance management is often seen as being about ensuring performance indicators are set and met. However, in social work, it is important that equal value is placed on the *way* that people work, so this needs to be taken into account in the setting of performance indicators.

Whilst supervision will provide useful evidence for the performance management framework, it is important to keep the balance and ensure that other areas are used in performance management.

How?

Performance management

- objective setting (agreeing the performance framework)
- agreeing skills and behaviour
- ensuring that objectives are met
- responding when performance doesn't meet objectives

Supervision

- learning
- support
- mediation
- accountability

(overlap)
- identifying learning plans
- coaching

Managing under performance

Having said that supervision is about more than performance management, where there are concerns about a practitioner's performance, these are likely to be addressed in the supervisory relationship. Highlighting areas where an individual is under performing can be difficult and some supervisors may try to avoid any potential conflict by not raising issues as they arise. However, this is most likely to lead to an escalation of any difficulties and ultimately a much more challenging situation.

Don't stick your head in the sand!

How?

Where there are any concerns about under performance, a supervisor needs to think about:

Are the expected standards set and clearly documented?

Does the practitioner understand the standards?

In what way are the standards not being met?

What are the reasons for the standards not being met?

123

The 'Difficult Conversation'

The supervisor must then be prepared to raise and discuss the issues with the practitioner. ACAS (2010) refer to this as having "that difficult conversation". In brief, the following agenda can be helpful to frame this discussion:

Clarify the practitioner's understanding of objectives and views on their performance

Ask the practitioner what they see as the objectives of their work and how they view their performance against each objective. Avoid the temptation to comment at this point - it will be helpful in step 2 to draw on the practitioner's comments.

Give your views on the individual's performance against the objectives

Ensure that you are specific and descriptive (giving concrete examples). Draw on any documentation that refers to objectives and on any evidence of the practitioner's performance.

How?

Explore any agreement (against each objective)
3 Highlight any areas where you agree.

Explore disagreements (against each objective)
4 Against each objective, highlight any areas of disagreement and try to establish reasons for the disagreements. Use facts and evidence to try to come to an agreement - if this is not possible, talk about how you might gather additional evidence.

Discuss the practitioner's strengths and learning needs
5 Highlight the practitioner's strengths to maintain a balance , then move to exploring where development is needed.

Agree an action plan with clear review dates
6 Make sure the plan is clear - who will do what? By when? and keep the plan under regular review.

Effective supervision: Putting the pieces together...

Developing best practice in supervision can be challenging for contemporary social work supervisors. However, putting the effort into providing effective supervision is well worth it because social workers who receive good quality supervision are:

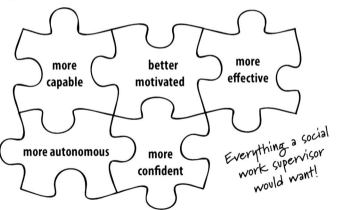

more capable

better motivated

more effective

more autonomous

more confident

Everything a social work supervisor would want!

How?

References

ACAS (2010) *How to Manage Performance*. (London) ACAS.

Atkin, G. and Weil, M. (1981) *The prior question: How do supervisors learn to supervise?* Social Coursework: The Journal of Contemporary Social Work, 62(8) pp. 472-479.

ANAS (2010) *Proposition de recommendation IFSW sure le burn out*. Available online at www.ifsw.org/p38002013.html. Accessed 2.11.10.

Berger, C. and Mizrahi, T. (2001) *An Evolving Paradigm of Supervision Within a Changing Health Care Environment*. Social Work in Health Care 32(4) pp. 1-8.

Billington, D. (1996) *Seven Characteristics of Highly Effective Adult Learning Programmes. New Horizons for Learning*. Available online at: www.newhorizons.org/lifelong/workplace/billington.htm. Accessed 12.1.08.

Bogo, M. and Dill, K. (2008) *Walking the tightrope: Using power and authority in Child Welfare Supervision*. Child Welfare 87(6) pp. 141-157.

Bowers, B., Esmond, S. and Canales, M. (1999) *Approaches to Case Management Supervision*. Administration in Social Work 23(1) pp. 24-49.

Brackett, J. (1904) *Supervision and Education in Charity*. (New York) Macmillan.

British Association of Social Workers (2011) *BASW / CoSW England Research on supervision in social work, with particular reference to supervision practice in multi-disciplinary teams*. (Birmingham) BASW.

Cherniss, C. and Goleman, D. (2001) *The Emotionally Intelligent Workplace*. (San Fransisco) Jossey Bass.

Children's Workforce Development Council and Skills for Care (2007) *Providing effective supervision: A workforce development tool, including a unit of competence and supporting guidance*. (Leeds) CWDC and Skills for Care.

Cohan, B. and Laufer, H. (1999) *The Influence of Supervision on Social Workers Perceptions of their Professional Competence*. The Clinical Supervisor 18 (2) pp. 39-50.

Community Care and Unison (2008) *Whatever Happened to Supervision?* Community Care April 23 2008.

How?

Dahlgren, L.O., Eriksson, B.E., Gyllenhammar, H., Korkeila, M., and Saaf-Rothoff, A. (2006) *To be and to have a critical friend in medical teaching.* Journal of Medical Education, 40 (1) pp. 5-6.

Davies, L. and Leonard, P. (Eds) (2004) *Social Work in a Corporate Era: Practices of Power and Resistance.* (Aldershot) Ashgate Publishing.

De Shazer, S. (1985) *Keys to Solution in Brief Therapy.* (New York) Norton.

Dempsey, M. (2011) *Control of Standards through appraisal, formal supervision, informal supervision and coaching.* Available online at: www.care-plan-management-system.co.uk/news/245/73/control-of-standards-through-appraisal-formal-supervision-informal-supervision-and-coaching. Accessed 25.11.11.

Dewane, C.J. (2007) *Supervisor Beware: Ethical Dangers in Supervision.* Social Work Today 7(4) pp. 34.

Dreyfus, H.L. and Dreyfus, S.E. (1986) *Mind over Machine: the power of human intuition and expertise in the era of the computer.* (Oxford) Basil Blackwell.

Eborall, C. and Garmeson, K. (2001) *Desk Research on Recruitment and Retention in Social Care and Social Work. Prepared for COI communications for the Department of Health.* Available online at: www.dh.gov.uk/dr_consum_dh/groups/dh_digitalassets/@en/documents/digitalasset/dh_4074320.pdf. Accessed 4.12.11.

Freeth, R. (2007) *Humanising Psychiatry and Mental Health Care: the challenge of the person-centred approach.* (Oxon) Radcliffe.

Grant, L. and Kinman, G. (2009) *Developing Emotional Resilience in Social Work Students: Supporting effective reflective practitioners.* Presentation at JSWEC Conference 2009.

Greenaway, R. (1995) *Powerful Learning Experiences in Management Learning and Development.* Available online at: http://reviewing.co.uk/research/ple_abs.htm. Accessed 21.9.10.

Harkness, D. and Hensley, H. (1991) *Changing the focus of social work supervision: effects on client satisfaction and generalised contentment.* British Journal of Social Work 36(6) pp. 506-512.

Hawkins, P. (2008) *Foreword to Passionate Supervision.* Edited by Shohet, R. (London) Jessica Kingsley Publishers.

Hawkins, P. and Shohet, R. (2006) *Supervision in the Helping Professions.* (3rd edition) (Berkshire) Open University Press.

Hennessey, R. (2011) *Relationship Skills in Social Work.* (London) Sage.

Henry, M. (2010) quoted in Hunter, M. (2010) *Solutions in Supervision.* Community Care 9.4.10.

Honey, P. and Mumford, A. (1982) *Manual of Learning Styles.* Peter Honey Publications.

Howe, D. (2008) *The Emotionally Intelligent Social Worker.* (Basingstoke) Palgrave Macmillan.

IFSW Europe (2011) *Charter of Rights for Social Workers.* (Berlin) IFSW Europe.

Inner London Probation Service (1993) *Working with Difference: A Positive and Practical Guide to Anti-Discriminatory Practice Teaching.* (London) Inner London Probation Service.

Jones, R. (2011) *The Glue that Binds*. Professional Social Work. February 2011. pp. 18-20.

Kadushin, A. (1992) *Supervision in Social Work*. (3rd Ed) (New York) Columbia University Press.

Kadushin, A. and Harkness, D. (2002) *Supervision in Social Work*. (4th Edition) (New York) Columbia Press.

Killian, J. and Todnem, G. (1991) *Reflective judgment concepts of justification and their relationship to age and education*. Journal of Applied Developmental Psychology, 2(2) pp. 89-116.

Kolb, D.A. (1984) *Experiential Learning: Experience as the Source of Learning and Development*. (New Jersey) Prentice Hall.

Lindsay, T. (2003) *An Investigation of group learning on practice placements*. The Higher Education Academy, Social Policy and Social Work (SWAP).

Livingstone, J. (2000) *Do you have problems with Recruitment and retention of staff? Responses to a survey of ARC members*. (Chesterfield) Association for Residential Care.

Magnuson, S., Norem, K. and Wilcoxon, S.A. (2000) *A Profile of Lousy Supervision. Experienced Counselors' perspectives.* Counselor Education and Supervision. 39(3) pp. 189-202.

Manchester City Council (2010) *Social Worker Recruitment and Retention (Manchester) Overview and Scrutiny Human Resources subgroup.* 12 January 2010.

McClure, P. (2002) *Reflection in Practice. Making Practice Based Learning Work.* (Ulster) University of Ulster.

Miller, J.F. and Powers, M.J. (1988) *Development of an Instrument to Measure Hope.* Nursing Research Vol 37(1) pp. 6-10.

Morrison, T. (2005) *Staff Supervision in Social Care: Making a Real Difference for Staff and Service Users.* (Brighton) Pavilion Publishing Ltd.

Munson, C.E. (2002) *Handbook of Clinical Social Work Supervision.* Third Edition (Binghampton) Haworth Social Work Press.

Noble, C. and Irwin, J. (2009) *Social Work Supervision: An exploration of the current challenges in a rapidly changing social, economic and political environment.* Journal of Social Work, Vol 9 (3) pp. 345-358.

O'Donoghue, K. (2000) *The future of social work supervision within Aoteraora/ New Zealand.* Presented at the National Supervision Conference. Supervision: From Rhetoric to Reality, July 2000, in the Auckland College of Further Education Available at: http://pages.prodigy.net/lizmitchell/volksware/ supervisionfuture.htm. Accessed 3.5.12.

O'Donoghue, K. (2012) *Uniprofessional, Multi-professional, Field of Practice, Discipline: Social Workers and Cross-disciplinary Supervision.* Available online at: http://massey.academia.edu/KieranODonoghue/Papers/877660/ Accessed 28.7.12.

Owen, H. and Pritchard, J. (1993) *Good practice in child protection: a manual for professionals.* (London) Jessica Kingsley.

Pack, M. (2009) *Clinical Supervision: An interdisciplinary review of literature with implications for reflective practice in social work.* Reflective Practice: International and Multidisciplinary Perspectives Vol 10 (5) pp. 657-668.

Petitt, B. and Olsson, H (1995) *Motespunker: nagra professionella verkty g l interktionistikk forandringsarbete.* (Stockholm) Mareld.

Pflieger, J. (2011) 8 characteristics that define relationship based work in reflective supervision. Available online at: http://eclkc.ohs.acf.hhs.gov/hslc/resources/professional%20Development/Staff%20Development/managers/health_fts_00525a_081205.html. Accessed 27.11.11.

Potter, C. and Brittain, C. (Ed) (2009) *Child Welfare Supervision: A Practical Guide for Supervisors, Managers and Administrators*. (Oxford) Oxford University Press.

Powell, D.J. and Brodsky, A. (1998) *Clinical Supervision in alcohol and drug abuse counselling: Principles, Models, Methods*. (San Francisco CA) Jossey Bass.

Ramos-Sanchez, L., Esmil, E., Goodwin, A., Riggs, S., Touster, L.O., Wright, L.K., Ratanasiripong, P. and Rodolfa, E. (2002) *Negative Supervisory events: Effects on supervision satisfaction and supervisory alliance*. Professional Psychology Research and Practice 33 pp. 107-202.

Rich, P. (2009) *Giving and Receiving Feedback*. Available online at: www.selfhelpmagazine.com/articles/growth/feedback.html. Accessed 10.9.09.

Rushton, A. and Nathan, J. (1996) *The Supervision of Child Protection Work*. The British Journal of Social Work 26 pp. 357-374.

Scaife, J. (2010) *Supervising the Reflective Practitioner: An essential guide to theory and practice.* (London) Routledge.

Schön, D. (1983) *The Reflective Practitioner: How Professionals think in action.* (London) Temple Smith.

Shulman, L. (1993) *Interactional Supervision.* (2nd Edition) (Washington) NASW Press.

Social Work Policy Institute (2011) *Supervision: The Safety Net for Front-Line Child Welfare Practice.* (Washington) National Association of Social Workers.

Social Work Reform Board (2010) *Building a Safe and Confident future: One year on.* (Crown Copyright) SWRB.

Social Work Reform Board (2011 online) *Standards for employers of social workers in England and Supervision Framework.* Available online at www.local.gov.uk/social-worker-standards. Accessed 4.12.11.

Stanford, S.N. (2011) *Constructing Moral Responses to Risk: A Framework for Hopeful Social Work Practice.* British Journal of Social Work Online March 24, 2011.

Stenhouse, L. (1975) *An Introduction to Curriculum Research and Development.* (London) Heinemann.

Stevenson, J. (2005) *Professional Supervision in Social Work.* Available online at www.unison-edinburgh.org.uk/socialwork/supervision.html. Accessed 15.10.11.

Stoltenberg, C.D., McNeill, B. and Delworth, U. (1998) *IDM Supervision: An Integrated Developmental Model of Supervising Counselors and Therapists.* (San Francisco) Jossey-Bass.

Tsui, M. (2005) *Social Work Supervision: Contexts and Concepts.* (London) Sage.

Waskett, C. (2006) *The Pluses of Solution Focussed Supervision.* Healthcare Counselling and Psychotherapy Journal Vol 6 (1) pp. 9-11.

Wonnacott, J. (2003) *The impact of supervision on child protection practice: a study of process and outcome.* University of Sussex. Unpublished dissertation.